Painting in towns and cities

Painting in towns and cities

Hans Schwarz

Studio Vista, London
Taplinger/Pentalic, New York

Acknowledgments

My thanks are due to Mr and Mrs S. Perring for kind permission to reproduce Fig. 82 and to Messrs Winsor & Newton for providing material used in Figs 7, 8, 11, 12, 13, 14, 16, 17 and the photograph Fig. 18. Figs 2 and 3 are reproduced by courtesy of the Trustees of the National Gallery, London, and Figs 4 and 5 by courtesy of the Trustees of the Tate Gallery, London. Fig. 4 Copyright SPADEM 1969. For Fig. 6 thanks are due to the Axel Springer Verlag.

A Studio Vista book
published by Cassell Ltd
35 Red Lion Square, London WC1R 4SG
and at Sydney, Auckland, Toronto, Johannesburg,
an affiliate of
Macmillan Publishing Co. Inc., New York

ISBN: 0 289 70973 3

Printed in Holland by Grafische Industrie Haarlem b.v.

Contents

Introduction

Our world is made up of buildings. They surround us. We live and work in them, and when we leave them we move on man-made surfaces – concrete and paving, tar and rails. Egyptian pyramids and medieval churches, Greek temples and Victorian railway stations, ancient universities and modern office blocks, schools, hospitals, factories, and a variety of domestic architecture, are our heritage.

No wonder architecture has been called the mother of all the arts. Every painting and drawing – even sculpture, graphic art and typography – have architectural elements of construction, weight, proportion. Buildings are basic to our imagination. A child's drawing of a house reveals his state of mind. The proportion and position of windows, the size of door and roof, even the size of the chimney and the amount of smoke coming out, show how happy, secure and well-adjusted he is. The house is the child, his universe. Buildings are not a cold, impersonal subject for a painter.

I must now declare my prejudices and limitations. My work is largely linear and tonal. Colour, though important, plays a second-ary role in my paintings. Ephemeral effects of light, however attractive, confuse the essential theme for me. I like to develop my paintings, changing my mind about colour and composition as I go along. Therefore I prefer to work from drawings in the studio. Also my oils are often bigger than could comfortably be painted out-of-doors. I know that sunlight, cast shadows and atmospheric effects are at the core of many artists' interest. Many painters work on a small scale, and so do not have the problem of carrying large canvases. Others feel that only an immediate approach can give their work the necessary freedom.

Further signs of my personal limitations will be apparent. Any advice I give, and any comment I make, will be coloured by my likes and dislikes. But then no artist, whether he is a teacher or not, can be without personal preferences. If he were, he would lack all enthusiasm and conviction.

Don't expect to be taught art in an objective way to a set standard, as one is taught mathematics. The best this book can do is to let you look while I draw and paint, and to let you listen while I talk to myself. Having my reasons, motives and reactions explained and analysed may help you to find your own style.

It is no bad thing if you find yourself influenced by my work and attitudes. In the search for a personal vision it is natural and healthy to be influenced by others, but in the end you are on your own and must decide for yourself what is right and wrong.

1　History

Realistic paintings of architecture and architectural detail decorated rooms in Pompeii two thousand years ago. But then, throughout the Middle Ages, paintings were meant to be read as symbols, and not to vie with physical reality. Even in descriptive works of art, like the Bayeux Tapestry, buildings are diagrammatic, flat patterns.

Only when we come near the Italian Renaissance do human and civic pride begin to create paintings of real towns. Charmingly toytown-like, in pink, pale blue and violet, these paintings none the less convey the exact feeling of the enclosed mediaeval city. Having looked at the murals in Florence (Fig. 1), and come out into the sunshine, the town around you – even with tourists and motor-cars – looks more like the fourteenth-century murals than the picture-postcards you send your friends.

To painters of the fifteenth century, like Uccello and Piero della Francesca, buildings were the ideal subject for displaying their mastery of perspective. The awakening interest in the antique also focused the artist's eye on the remains of Roman architecture. But these architectural settings were of *invented*, not real, buildings.

The paintings were pervaded by a clear, neutral light. Neither hard sunshine nor mist affects the clarity with which we see their imagined world.

It was northern artists around 1500, Dürer foremost among them, who were the first to take their sketchbooks and water-colours out-of-doors; taking note of clouds, sun, mist and the accidents of time and decay.

Dutch and Flemish painters of the seventeenth century provided faithful views of their towns and houses for proud burghers. There were interiors of bright, clean churches (Fig. 2), and of rowdy taverns. Servants sweep already sparkling tiled halls under the eye of their well-starched mistresses. Perspective was impeccable, light and shade so well observed that we can tell the season, even the time of day.

In Italy, archaeological interest and the tourist industry (in the seventeenth and eighteenth centuries every well-born young man was expected to go on the Grand Tour) encouraged a school of painters and engravers of views of towns, temples and ruins. Reprints of Piranesi's dramatic etchings of Roman ruins and churches are sold today from Roman book-stalls. Canaletto's views of Venice (Fig. 3) are still held in high regard - reproductions of his paintings have been amongst the most popular for many years now. Every trick and device was used to give vivid verisimilitude.

Fig 1

Fig 2   *St Bavo, Haarlem* by Saenredam. National Gallery, London

The Camera Obscura, the forerunner of our photographic camera, gave an exact projection of optical appearances, from which to trace the outlines. Brush ruling and ruling pens defined the detail; calculated scumbles and glazes added texture to wall and paving. In spite of these impersonal proceedings, the paintings are full of eighteenth-century grace and spirit.

The young Turner, Bonnington and David Cox (Fig. 4), and other English artists of the early nineteenth century, were influenced by the Italians. But watercolour was their chosen medium, and atmosphere was important to them. However grand and impressive the depicted buildings were, their work has an intimate cosiness.

Whatever their style, the intention of all these artists was informative and documentary. They wanted the spectator to see what a scene or a building looked like. When, in the middle of the nineteenth century, photography freed the artist from this role of

Fig 3 *The Stonemason's Yard* by Canaletto. National Gallery, London

reporter, painters began to think more of their personal reactions to what they saw. Whether an Impressionist painted a haystack or the Houses of Parliament, his concern lay with what colours the object reflected and how light and shade were related, and not in any intrinsic beauty or interest of the object.

To Cézanne, and later the Cubists, the painting itself is a structure, with architectural qualities of volume and solidity, regardless of the actual subject.

Utrillo was born and lived in the Paris streets he painted with such feeling (Fig. 5). The crumbling plaster of the tenements is matched exactly by his technique – in fact he used plaster, sand, sawdust to give texture to his paint-surface. As he was not a facile draughtsman, he used postcard photographs as references and to sort out problems of perspective and foreshortening.

Van Gogh's writhing and rearing bright yellow houses, with lilac roofs against deep ultramarine skies, began the Expressionist

Fig 4 *Near the Pont d'Arcole, Paris* by David Cox. Tate Gallery, London

movement. At first sight buildings seem hard, neutral, unsympathetic subjects for this personal, heightened art. But it was exactly these cool subjects that released the fiercest emotions.

I find Kokoschka's townscapes of sweeping, panoramic views the most exciting paintings of buildings. London, New York and Berlin (Fig. 6), are among the towns he painted, yet he treated small places, for instance Polperro in Cornwall, in the same majestic way. Usually done from a height, in bright sparkling, broken colour, the subtly distorted perspective – similar to that achieved by the fish-eye (very wide angle) lens in photography – gives one a feeling of being totally enclosed and involved in the environment.

In Lowry's work, black and white predominate. The drawing is artlessly simple and the compositions are flat and stark. With the simplest of means he turns the harsh surroundings of the industrial north into moving works of art.

Whenever you feel that the available subjects are not picturesque or interesting enough to paint from, think of this painter and of how he deals with drab, unpromising material.

Fig 5   *Place du Tertre* by Utrillo. Tate Gallery, London

Fig 6   *Berlin 1966* by Kokoschka. Axel Springer Verlag

2 Materials

Pencil, chalk and pen

Pencil drawing is often thought to be an unsympathetic medium. This is partly because a hard (usually labelled H) pencil is often used, from fear that a soft one (usually labelled B) would smudge too easily. Don't worry about that – a tidy drawing is not necessarily a good one. Even for fine detail a B-pencil, well sharpened and used lightly, is better than an H-pencil, pressed on hard.

Do not mix different degrees of pencils in one drawing – such as an HB for the outline and a 6B for the shading. It invariably looks wrong.

The usual lead (or rather graphite) pencil always has a silvery sheen – even a 6B. There are a number of other drawing pencils – charcoal pencils, carbon pencils, Conté pencils, Chinagraph pencils. All these give a juicy, black line.

Conté crayons, wood-cased or in stick-form, come in several degrees of hardness in black, white, red or brown. Wood-cased crayons have advantages; they can be sharpened easily, held conveniently and they keep your hands clean. But the solid chalk or crayon can be used laid on its side, giving a wide sweep

Fig 7

Fig 8

of tone, and is probably preferable for large and bold drawings (Fig. 7).

Attempts to mix pencil and Conté in the same drawing are inadvisable. Apart from aesthetic considerations, Conté crayon does not draw on top of graphite, or any greasy surface.

Black litho crayon is made for use on stone or metal plates for the production of lithographic prints. It is obtainable in several degrees of hardness and has a similar quality on paper to wax crayon.

Charcoal smudges, or indeed dusts off, easily; yet it is the ideal medium for free, bold sketches. Because of its softness and bluntness, its versatility and character can only be appreciated when it is used on a large scale.

Pastels are made in a range of several hundred colours. They are very fragile, liable to smudge, and must either be glazed or sprayed with fixative, which impairs their bloom. Tinted, soft-surfaced paper, such as Ingres paper or Strathmore charcoal paper, is the most sympathetic support for pastels.

Oil pastels and oil crayons are excellent colour media in their own right. Although they can be dissolved with turpentine and worked on with a brush, they should not be thought of as a cheap substitute for oil paint (Fig. 8).

15

Oil pastels do not smudge, but they don't have the bloom of traditional pastels. They are cheap; a box containing the full range of sixty colours costs about £2 ($4).

Oil crayons are harder, not as opaque, but more precise drawings can be done with them.

Pens like Gillot 303 are specially designed for the artist. Although I used them for many years, I now find them hard and unsympathetic. Some fountain-pen nibs are more responsive. One pen, or rather series of pens, which I find most useful, is the Rapidograph (Fig. 9). It is a fountain-pen with a nib which is a fine tube, with a needle valve regulating the flow of ink from the reservoir. Interchangeable tips allow different thicknesses of line. I prefer the wider nibs, the fine ones can be scratchy. The Rapidograph, and other pens working on the same principle, take a little getting used to. One has to draw with the pen held almost at right angles to the paper and the line is of even thickness, whatever the pressure. An obvious advantage it shares with all fountain pens is that you needn't bother with bottles of ink when drawing out-of-doors.

Fig 9

Some years ago I went out to sketch and found that I had come without a pen of any sort. But I had an old watercolour brush in my pocket. With a penknife I cut the brush handle into a chisel-edge (Fig. 10). I now use this device regularly, and many of the drawings reproduced in this book were done with it (Figs 51, 54, 55, 59, etc.). The 'pen' holds little ink and has to be dipped frequently. Another disadvantage is that one often has to re cut the drawing edge. On the other hand, you can cut exactly the width and thickness that suits the current drawing.

There are a number of traditional natural pens: quill pens, bamboo and reed pens – but I prefer my brush handle!

Indian ink is dense black and waterproof, so washes of colour can be put over it without blurring. But it clogs the nib and has a viscous, greasy drag. This can be overcome, however, by thinning the ink with distilled water.

Black Pelikan Fount India is nearly as black as waterproof indian ink, without its disadvantages. However many artists use ordinary writing ink – black, blue or any colour they fancy – to draw with.

Fig 10

Fig 11

Ball point pens have a sharp, thin line, which is dead-looking. The marks made by felt and fibre nibs have a second-hand look, as though they were photostatted. This is because of the instant-drying dye these pens contain.

Many quick sketches are done only to provide information for paintings to be done later. However, they are your direct reaction to a subject, and are bound to influence the character of the ultimate painting. Therefore the technique used for them should be sympathetic – felt pens and ball points are not.

Pen can be used on the same drawing with pencil and crayon, each contributing its character. But pen should never be used carefully to trace and fill in a preliminary faint pencil drawing. If you use a pen, use it courageously. Every line, at whatever stage of the drawing, should be a thinking, probing line.

Bank (mimeograph) or duplicating paper, held with a rubber band or a clip to a piece of hardboard or thick cardboard, makes an excellent sketch book. The rigid backing is important. In a limp sketch book a piece of stiff board can be inserted behind the sheet you draw on. Apart from stiffening it, this avoids the transfer of the pressure of your pen or pencil to subsequent clean pages.

Sketchbooks of cartridge (drawing) paper are expensive, and often contain only twenty sheets of paper. Layout pads (sketch-pads) and so-called students' sketchbooks (Fig. 11), are preferable.

Fig 12

Watercolour, coloured ink, gouache and mixed techniques

This list of colours will serve for any medium – watercolour, gouache, acrylic or oils, except that with the last three, opaque, media you will also need white:
Alizarin crimson
Cobalt blue (or winsor blue, thalo blue or prussian blue, which is fierce and should be used with restraint).
Cadmium yellow.

With these three pigments alone, the primaries, it is possible in theory to mix every colour – but only in theory. You will also need:

Viridian and ultramarine. Colours which extend the range of green and blue.

Yellow ochre, raw sienna, burnt sienna, raw umber, burnt umber. These are earth colours and, although dull, they have definite uses and character.

Finally, you will need black, although some painters and teachers deny the need for it and will not allow their students to use it. But look at the work of painters from Rembrandt to Manet and Picasso to see how beautifully it can be used.

Metal watercolour boxes can be bought fitted with either tubes or pans of colours; or the boxes can be bought empty. They are useful; there is a space for brushes and the lid and flap serve

Fig 13

as a palette (Fig. 12). I would advise buying the box only, and fitting it with your own selection of colours – preferably tubes. Colours in pans have to be loosened with a moist brush, and unless you are very meticulous, they easily get contaminated with the colour already in the brush. The trouble of loosening generous brushfuls also tends to make you paint stingily.

Watercolours are intended to be used as washes, leaving the paper, the support, to provide the light tones. Waterproof coloured inks (Fig. 13), are even more transparent and luminous. Being waterproof, layer after layer can be put on, gaining in depth and intensity, without going dull or muddy. If thinned with tap-water (the makers recommend distilled or rain water), they sometimes curdle and go gluey, or deposit a sediment. This can actually be exploited, to give a variety of texture.

Very few bottles are needed to give a wide range by mixing. Crimson, prussian blue, yellow, violet and emerald, together with a bottle of black indian ink should be enough. The great drawback is that the colours are not permanent. All waterproof inks fade.

Gouache is opaque watercolour. It is also called bodycolour, and, in its cheaper version, postercolour. Jars, tubes and pans are on the market, and again tubes (Winsor and Newton's Designers' Colours are recommended) are the most convenient (Fig. 14). Its

20

Fig 14

opacity allows corrections and second thoughts. Remember that colours sometimes dry lighter than they were when wet. Also, earlier layers can dissolve and affect the colour subsequently applied.

To make gouache waterproof, mix a drop of acrylic medium with the paint as you use it. Certain plastic adhesives, such as Unibond (U.K.) or Elmer's glue (U.S.), serve the same purpose.

Plastic-bound colours themselves – acrylic and PVA (polymer) colours – are completely water-, and anything else, proof. Only water is needed to paint with them. They dry nearly as quickly as gouache. Be careful, if you let them dry in a brush you will never get it clean again.

All the techniques so far dealt with in this chapter are inter-mixable. A drawing may begin in pencil, pen may be added, watercolour and waterproof ink can be superimposed, accents of oil pastels and patches of gouache or acrylic paint will complete it. I think it is the solemn respect commanded by watercolour as a pure medium, in particular, that is responsible for much dead and timid work.

Hog-hair (called bristle in U.S.) brushes can be used, but sable, the usual watercolour brushes, seem best suited to these media. Do not be stingy; a good quality brush carries out your intentions fluidly and precisely. A cheap brush has to be fought, or at least coaxed, all the way. A good brush is justified as an economy. A good big brush has a fine point which will do for detail, so you need fewer brushes. It also lasts far longer than a cheap one.

Cotman, Whatman, D'Arches and Fabriano watercolour papers are traditionally used for these media. There are various thick-nesses and qualities of smooth- and rough-surfaced cartridge paper or other sturdy, white drawing paper. I often use Kent paper, or Turkey Mill as it is also called. It is pure white and has a finely textured, rough surface. But some painters find this paper glaring and hard.

There are many other, less usual, papers that give interesting results. Thick Japanese tissue-paper makes pen lines and washes spread softly. Blotting paper and newsprint have similar effects. Cheap papers like poster paper and lining paper also give ink and paint a blotchy edge.

Thick brown wrapping paper, strawboard and buff Manila give character to drawings and paintings by their colour and qualities. China-clay coated, glossy printing paper, called art paper in U.K., absorbs ink and washes in sharply defined areas, giving a hard edge to each brush mark.

Some of these cheap papers have disadvantages; they fade or yellow with age, others fuzz if an eraser is used on them.

You may have to buy these papers from a printer or a paper merchant. Buying from them is invariably cheaper than buying from an art store. I have always found them helpful and generous, even if I only wanted a few sheets of paper. But if you find a paper that suits you, it is worth buying in quantity.

There is no need for heavy or expensive drawing boards. Any rigid, smooth board, plywood or even hardboard, will do to draw on. Clips or drawing pins (thumb tacks) will hold your paper.

All paper, unless it approaches cardboard in thickness, will stretch, undulate, cockle or buckle, when wet washes are applied. If you are concerned about this, you can stretch it:

Wet the paper generously all over with a sponge. Leave it for a little to allow it to expand. Then attach it to the board with strips of brown gum adhesive tape all around (Fig. 15).

Fig 15

When dry, the paper will be taut and stay so, however wetly you paint. Winsor & Newton make a sketching frame, Bell's Watercolour Sketching Frame, which does the same job, holding the wetted paper with clips and strips of wood. But it is made only in one rather small size – 10" × 14" (inside dimensions). It is not available in the U.S. but can be specially ordered.

22

Fig 16

Oils

Apart from the colours mentioned on page 19, you will need white. I use zinc white, or titanium white which is more brilliant but a little less smooth. I also use a semi-prepared decorators' titanium white which is less greasy, a little thinner and dries matt in a matter of hours. Foundation white (also a British product) has a similar quality, as do the various underpainting whites available from American manufacturers.

Buy colours in large tubes, particularly white, which you use most.

There are well over a hundred colours made by each manufacturer. So try other colours; you must discover your own range. Your sense of colour must find its own expression with whatever pigments suit you best.

Turpentine is the traditional medium for oil paint, but turps substitute, also called white spirits or mineral spirits – does the job equally well, at a fraction of the price. All it has to do is to thin the paint – as water does in watercolour and gouache – and, like water, to evaporate completely. It also cleans your brushes. Buy it by the pint from a hardware or paint store.

If you paint thinly, some linseed oil can be added to give body to the paint and to make it less fragile in thin layers.

Watercolour or gouache paintings can be done with one brush, but for oils you need more. Start off with at least six brushes (Fig. 16): five hog-hair or bristle brushes – a 1″ and a ½″ flat, a ½″ and a ¼″ filbert, a $\frac{3}{16}$″ round – and a pointed sable, an old watercolour brush will do.

When you have finished painting for the day, wash brushes first in white (mineral) spirits, then in soap or detergent, stroking the brush back and forth on the palm, rinsing under the tap and repeating till the brush is clean.

Any hard, smooth, non-absorbent surface can be used as a palette. Wood, glass, metal, enamel or Formica will serve, even paper; expendable, tear-off palettes are useful for out-door painting. Get used to squeezing colours (in generous amounts) always in the same order around the edge of the palette, leaving the centre for mixing.

I paint on hardboard (untempered Masonite), primed with white undercoating. Emulsion paint can also be used for priming. If you like to work on a coloured surface, you can use under-coating or emulsion of any colour. A coat of glue, size, PVC adhesive, such as Unibond, or acrylic gesso or Permalba-Latex gesso (U.S.) will seal the surface, without altering its colour. These sealers dry in a few hours, undercoating takes about twelve hours. Prepare whole 8' × 4' sheets and saw off pieces for indi-vidual paintings.

Use the smooth side of hardboard. The textured side may seem reminiscent of canvas, but its deep pits and hard ridges give paintings an unpleasantly coarse look.

Hardboard is permanent, cheap, rigid, and universally obtain-able; yet canvas is still thought by many artists the ideal support. Ready-primed canvas can be bought in many qualities. Winsor & Newton, for instance, make six different qualities and textures, each in four to six different widths, a choice of thirty-two in all. Canvas can also be bought ready for painting on stretchers in about thirty different sizes. Or you can stretch the canvas your-self on stretchers, which come in sizes from 5" to 5'.

Money can be saved by preparing your own canvas with size and undercoating, or with white lead in oil (U.S.). Acrylic gesso is even easier to use for preparing canvases.

Canvas can be pinned (tacked) to a board, or even a wall, for painting. But for framing it will have to be stretched or glued to a panel of wood or hardboard.

There are various proprietory canvasboards, oil-sketching papers and painting blocks. Paper can be painted on, even with-out priming – tracing paper is particularly suitable. Wood panels, cardboard, plywood, silk and leather have been used: stone, glass, metal and ivory have been painted on.

3 General

Watercolours, new and revolutionary in 1800, still exert a pull over some amateur artists. The brilliant light and thick oil paint of Impressionist painting a hundred years ago find dreary echoes today in views of Paris boulevards and fishing villages reflected in the harbour. Some pen and pencil drawings still look back nostalgically to eighteenth-century vistas and prospects.

Not only style and technique but also subjects are often chosen timidly and conventionally. My first experience of amateur art was in the industrial Midlands of England. The paintings never reflected the rough, exciting and vital Black Country around us. They were of pretty thatched cottages and idyllic nooks and crannies. Later in London I rarely saw a painting of crowded streets and piled buildings; no, picturesque scenes again, in the Home Counties and the Costa Brava.

This seems wrong; picture-postcard views don't necessarily make beautiful paintings. The more conventionally acceptable a subject, the more difficult it is to escape a conventional and hackneyed interpretation. The more ordinary the subject, the easier it is to be personal and creative in one's reaction.

Though you may be puzzled by the work of some *avant-garde* artists, look at their work and try to understand it. Much modern art, and abstract art in particular, is concerned with problems of construction, composition and balance in a way which closely links it to architecture.

Painting is never – and never has been – just a copying in a photographic way. The more slavishly you copy, the less likely are you to discover your own style and vision. The ostensible subject may only be an excuse. For instance my use of buildings as subject matter means that through them I can indulge in compositions based on a division of the picture into rectangles, which appeals to me. It also allows me to use certain muted colours – greys and browns – which I find sympathetic.

And the often-heard argument that one ought to learn to draw 'properly' before developing one's own style is, I am sure, false. There can be no generally accepted way of drawing 'properly'. The only proper way to draw and paint is in one's own personal idiom, and not by learning dry tricks and techniques.

If you start to paint and draw, perhaps years after having done any so-called art at school, you may feel isolated and in need of contact with other artists. There are correspondence courses and books (like this), but however good they are, half an hour with a live artist is better than all the books in the library.

The solution is to join a group or a class. They are either run by local education authorities in Britain, by adult education centres in America, or privately by established artists, advertized in art magazines and periodicals. Fees, particularly in the case of education authority or adult education centre classes, are minimal.

In the summer months there are residential courses, some for a week or longer, others for only a weekend, with tutors and visiting lecturers.

Many artists give private and group tuition, and there is probably an art society within a few miles of your home. Don't feel that you are not 'good' enough to join in any of these. Nearly every member or student in these groups, classes or societies felt that, until he joined and found every member thinking the same about himself.

You are unlikely to find a class specifically concerned with the painting or drawing of buildings, but there are landscape classes, and particularly in summer many groups go out to draw and paint; the choice of subject is left to you. Anyhow, whether you paint a figure, a still life or a street scene, the technique is the same and the problems of light, proportion, composition and perspective are related.

Although the back of an envelope and a stub of pencil will serve to make notes for a painting, it is a good idea to get into the habit of carrying a small sketch book, a pencil, pen, eraser and crayon in your pocket. I also use two bigger sketch books, one 10"×8", the other 14"×9".

For larger, more elaborate, work I carry a 15"×22" board (half-imperial) in a portfolio, with a selection of different papers and art boards. If you do more than one drawing at a session, a change of paper and technique is refreshing and can keep you from getting into a routine.

In a small rucksack I have six bottles of coloured ink, as many tubes of gouache, a box of oil pastels and crayons, a pencil box with pens, brushes, pencil, razor blade, eraser (never used), a screw-top jar with water, some rag and a few tobacco tins to use as palettes (Fig. 17).

If you work in one medium only, it is simpler. You only need, say, a watercolour box, a few brushes, water bottle, sponge and rag. Nor does painting in oils out-of-doors mean vast equipment. Stretched canvas, a block of oil paper or a piece of prepared hard-

Fig 17

board, a dozen tubes of paint, brushes, palette and palette knife, white (mineral) spirits, a dipper (ladle or cup), rag and some charcoal are all you need. They can all be carried neatly in a wooden or metal oil painting box, or equally well – If less tidily – in any bag or case. To carry wet oil paintings, there are canvas pins made which hold two canvases apart from each other. The traditional image of the wandering landscape painter, carrying easel, canvases, stool, sunshade and vast paint box, is fading. If you paint architecture you are unlikely to be far from a road. You can use a car as a mobile studio, and wet oil paintings can be carried in the back, face up.

I have painted sitting on the roof of my station waggon (denting the roof), and crouched in the back if it rained. I have painted in the driver's seat, the board on the steering wheel, every vigorous line sounding the horn. The car is also useful if you feel awkward about working in full view of passers-by.

If you do intend using a sketching easel, get a firm one (Fig. 18), the sturdier the better. Your painting is a good sail, and quite a slight breeze can blow over even a hefty easel. So if there is any wind, it is wise to anchor the easel with a rope to a stone.

Although I rely on public benches, kerb-stones (curbs) and low walls, and of course the car, I often wish that I carried a folding stool.

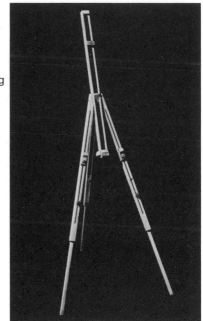

Fig 18

A frame, or even only a mount (called a mat in America) on a drawing or watercolour make an enormous difference. But this book is not the place to go into detailed instruction (nor am I a good enough framer to give them). So, here are just a few hints.

Drawings and watercolours usually have a mount (mat) between picture and frame. The bigger the drawing, the wider the mount (mat). Usually they are the same width at the sides and the top, but a little deeper at the bottom. Don't use cardboard that is very bright in colour, or colours that too obviously echo a dominant colour in your picture.

It does not take a great deal of skill to cut reasonably neat mounts (mats). You will need a steel-edge ruler and a very sharp knife, a Stanley knife, as well as a board and plenty of old cardboard to do the cutting on.

Without a special mount-cutting (mat) knife it is a little tricky to cut bevelled mounts (mats). But it can be done, as long as the knife is not held at too sloping an angle (Fig. 19). Beyond an angle of about 60° the point of the knife is likely to leave the guiding ruler. The thicker the card (matting material), the deeper and wider the bevel, the lusher will be the look of the picture.

Fig 19

But even a thin mount (mat), with a straight, vertically-cut opening will improve the look of your work and protect it.

Cut the opening of the mount (mat) at least half an inch smaller than the drawing, or the edges of the drawing may creep through the mount (mat) and get creased and dog-eared. Sellotape (Scotch tape) will secure at top and bottom to the back of the mount. A piece of cardboard, the full size of the mount (mat), pasted behind the drawing, will further strengthen and protect it. Some artists put cellophane over drawing and mount, securing it with adhesive tape at the back; though this seems of use only if the drawing is likely to get a lot of handling.

As with drawing paper, you are likely to get a bigger, and cheaper, selection of cardboard at a paper merchant or large printer than at an art supplies store.

If you have your work framed professionally, don't go to a shop which acts as an agent. Give it directly to the framer, with whom you can decide on the best finish, colour, size etc.

We all have a few old frames in the attic, and friends, from the kindest motives, try to give us theirs. But unless they are in

Fig 20

brand-new condition and really suitable, it is better not to be tempted. Ribbed Edwardian frames with bits of plaster broken away are not miraculously transformed by a coat of paint, however bright, even if you add sand or sawdust to it.

To make your own frames from lengths of moulding, you will need a mitre-block (miter box). However careful you are, without one it is impossible to make a clean 45° saw-cut. To tack and glue the corners a mitre clamp is also a great help.

Half-round, square or bevelled mouldings (Fig. 20), about 1" wide, are the most suitable for drawings and watercolours in mounts (mats). They look well in natural wood, gilt, or a neutral, light colour. Around oil paintings too, simple frames, though somewhat deeper and weightier, look best.

A frame ought not to assert itself or turn the picture into a tasteful bit of decoration.

Traditional framing is not the only way of presenting drawings and paintings. Drawings, prints and watercolours are put behind glass, which is held to a hardboard or plywood backing or to a second sheet of glass with clips or metal strips. Frames are made of aluminium angle or Perspex (Plexiglass). Oil paintings are edged with narrow metal or wood *baguettes* (rounded strips), or with coloured Sellotape or Scotch tape around the thickness of the stretchers. Paintings are sunk in boxes or raised on blocks. And if you can't face the trouble of framing, remember that some museums have done away with frames altogether and even old master paintings are hung naked and exposed.

Local and national societies hold open exhibitions; competitions and theme exhibitions are advertized in art periodicals. If you have work which you think worth showing, send for submission forms. They give details of fees, dates and conditions.

Apart from the obvious pleasure of having your work seen and the unlikely chance of having it bought, to see your own painting among others is instructive. Parts which you thought bold look tame alongside other paintings. Your painting seems to shrink. You can nearly see yourself as others see you. And incidentally, by this comparison you gain insight into fellow-exhibitors' thought and technique.

If you go to the trouble of submitting your work, you want to see it hung. It hurts having it rejected. You may well feel that worse paintings than yours were accepted. That does not mean that the selection committee are a collection of unprincipled crooks who hang their own and their friends' work. I have served on many selection committees, and may have allowed work to hang which did not deserve it and have rejected better, but to go through masses of work and keep a completely even standard of judgment is difficult.

Don't let rejection discourage you. Go on painting and submit your work again. However discouraged you may be at the moment, it is not humiliating. It happens to all of us. You can be certain that every member of the hanging committee himself had work rejected in more than one show. Even if you find yourself repeatedly un-hung, remember that ultimately one paints for oneself, one's own pleasure, the good of one's own soul.

But when your painting is thought good enough to hang in an exhibition and someone (even if it is a friend) thinks it good enough to hang in his own home, then it is worth a reasonable price. The compliment paid us by having our work in their home is thought by some people to be at least part-payment. No manufacturer will let me have his product cheaper because he is flattered at my having chosen his goods.

Fig 21

4 Perspective

I persuaded three teenagers of no more than average talent and skill to draw the same quite complex building (Fig. 21); I too drew the same subject (Fig. 22).

Now, I think that the teenagers' drawings are well-composed and decorative. The textures of tiles, bricks, window panes and leaves fill the spaces of their drawings admirably. The mistakes they made in perspective do not detract from the quality of their drawings. But they themselves were troubled by these mistakes.

All three made the same mistakes – they drew edges which in fact appear to run down, running up. For a simple reason – when

Fig 22

one asks anyone to draw a cube, this (Fig. 23), is what they draw, never this (Fig. 24). One always imagines that one is looking *down* on objects, never up at them. So receding edges, A–B, A–C, are drawn rising *upwards*. But only receding lines *below* your eye-level appear to *rise*. Lines *above* the eye-level, and in a building many lines are above, seem to *descend* as they recede (Fig. 25).

The rule underlying this can be framed: all parallel horizontal lines seem to converge on the same vanishing point at eye-level (Fig. 26). The lines above eye-level (A, B, C) seem to descend, those below (D, E, F) seem to rise.

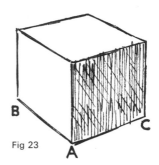

Fig 23

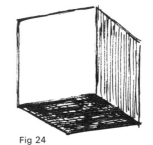

Fig 24

Fig 25

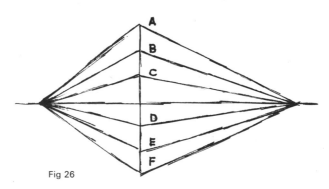

Fig 26

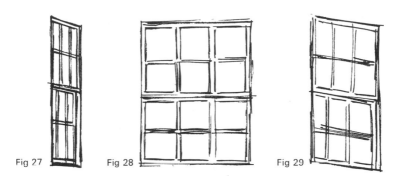

Fig 27 Fig 28 Fig 29

My three youngsters also exaggerated the width of fore-shortened surfaces. A window appears like this (Fig. 27), but they *knew* that it is like Fig. 28 in elevation. So it was obvious to draw half what they saw and half what they knew, to compromise (Fig. 29).

The apparent width of a fore-shortened receding plane can be checked against a pencil or brush, with your thumb marking the proportions (Fig. 30).

Fig 30

It is a related common mistake to exaggerate the size of top surfaces of bodies below the eye-level – a stool looking like this (Fig. 31), will often be drawn like this (Fig. 32). Again, by using your thumb against the pencil, you can check depth of A–B against B–C. You may well get a surprise at finding how very shallow A–B really is.

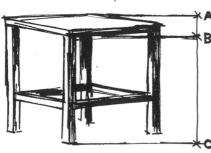

Fig 31

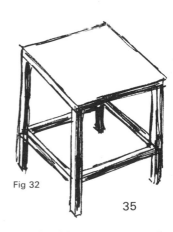

Fig 32

35

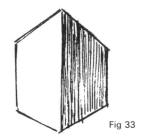

Fig 33

The larger and closer any object appears – building, window, chair, any object – the more fiercely will it foreshorten and seem to slope away (Fig. 33). Get further away and it will look like this (Fig. 34). From still further away there will hardly be any perceptible slope in the horizontal edges (Fig. 35). The reason for this has nothing to do with the *size* of the object or with the *distance* it is away from you. Near or large objects do not obey different laws of perspective from far or small objects. It is entirely dependent on how much of your field of vision an object occupies.

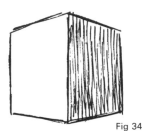

Fig 34

A large house in the distance can appear much smaller – and therefore less distorted – than the small window through which you see it (Fig. 36), but if their edges run parallel they will share the same vanishing point.

Fig 35

If you are faced with regular subdivisions of receding planes, such as a tiled floor or the glazing bars (the frames which hold the panes of glass) in a window, it may help to remember that diagonals determine the apparent halfway points (Fig. 37). This same trick, and it is no more than that, may also help with the distribution of windows in a facade or the placing of the apex in a gable end (Fig. 38).

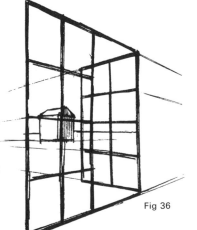

Fig 36

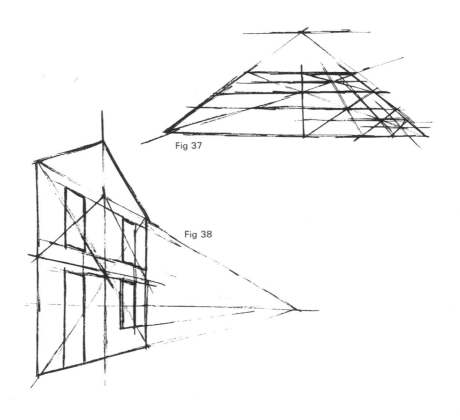

Fig 37

Fig 38

I have written about windows, stools, tiles and gables. But the same laws apply to all surfaces and solid bodies. For instance, the example of the exaggerated top surface of the stool in Figs 31–2 may explain to you why road surfaces in your paintings have a habit of rising and rearing rather than lying flat.

Problems of perspective must be responsible for many people's reluctance to draw or paint buildings, streets and architectural subjects. But the importance of perspective is often exaggerated. Try not to be bothered by it.

Perspective is only an artificial device to accommodate an illusion of three dimensions on the two dimensions of your picture. Perspective is not 'truth', it is distortion. For instance, a square drawn in perspective retains none of the characteristics of squares – four right-angles and four sides of equal length.

Before the fifteenth century the word perspective did not exist, and some wonderful pictures of buildings and townscapes were painted.

5 Drawing

The artist who chooses townscapes and architecture as his subject must draw. The life of a town – people, cars, dogs, bicycles, buses – has to be captured speedily. Figs 39, 40, 41 are examples of this. They are drawn in pencil, 2B or softer, on smooth paper, about 8″×10″.

Fig 40   *Strand on the Green*

The cyclist in the sky in Fig. 39 is not a flight of fancy. There just wasn't room on the ground. The three dogs in Fig. 40, are the same dog, drawn as it moved about. Nor did the variety of incident in Fig. 41 happen at the same moment – even if it had, no one could record it, however rapid a sketcher. People sitting on benches, taking dogs for walks, feeding swans, rowing on the river, children watching and climbing the embankment – all this was in constant movement. These changes in the scene may suggest better compositions, and often it is necessary to do many drawings of the subject.

Even if you consider yourself weak in figure drawing, try to get the feeling of busy-ness in this kind of subject. Likeness, proportion, anatomy are not important. Just look at the stick figures with which Utrillo and Lowry people their towns.

Could you draw a telephone kiosk (booth) from memory? Or a lamp post? How about a park bench, a letter box (mailbox) or a traffic light? These characteristic objects, street furniture as they are called, add conviction to a setting. Think of the variety of iron railings (Figs 40, 41, 42, 43 and 56).

Fig 39   *Camden Town*

39

Fig 41   *Putney Embankment*

You may decide in the painting you do from sketches to simplify, or even to do away with, some of these impedimenta. But draw them in the first place with some precision; they can't be invented or reconstructed from insufficiently-defined drawings.

Lettering is another constant in urban environment. Posters, road signs, shop signs surround us. The greyhound stadium (Fig. 44), built of corrugated iron, breeze blocks (cinder blocks),

Fig 42 *Hammersmith Bridge*

boarding and asbestos sheeting is an affront to town planning and architecture. But its unexpected angles, its planes and textures, and in particular the wild use of lettering, make it an exciting subject. Would-be modern, eye-catching letter-forms signal urgent messages from every facet. The distorted and foreshortened words on the receding surfaces add further interest.

  In contrast, all the lettering in Fig. 45 – posters, road signs, shop

Fig 43

Fig 44

Fig 45   *York Road, Wandsworth*

and pub signs – are facing you squarely, parallel to the picture
plane. These precise rectangles, echoing the rectangle of the
drawing, act as a steadying influence in the design. In Fig. 46 the
foreground interest is an elaborate road name plate. Its juicy
Victorian baroque contrasts with the harsh Black Country background.

This drawing was later used for a painting, hence the squaring-
up. The equivalent network, based on diagonals, was drawn on the
canvas, making sure that the proportions were exactly as on the
drawing – 11" × 8" became 44" × 32". The network on the drawing
is in coloured pencil, to avoid confusion. On the canvas the network is drawn in charcoal and the lay-in of the drawing is done in
oil paint with a fine brush. As soon as this is dry the charcoal
can be dusted off. Paintings of elaborate subjects, such as townscapes, are often transferred from drawings by means of squaring-
up. Usually all signs of this are eliminated. But some artists,
W. R. Sickert was one, allow the network to remain visible on
the finished painting.

Even now, with photography the obvious means of documentary illustration, books on architecture often employ drawings
when precise information about details of mouldings and proportion are demanded. A drawing can be selective and, of course,

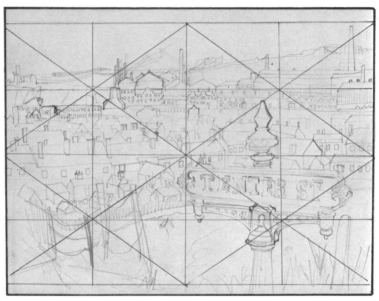

Fig 46   *Halesowen, Worcestershire*

can convey the spirit in a way which is impossible for the camera. When some of the bombed buildings in Europe were rebuilt after the last war, old drawings were of more use to the architects than the many photographs that were available.

The drawings in Figs 41, 42, 43, 47, 48 and 49 were done with the intention of giving precise information about detail of structure and texture. A sharp pencil, an HB, was used.

It might have been more telling and decorative if I had drawn the facade in Fig. 43 as a flat elevation, without any foreshortening; and Fig. 47 also might have been better if approached entirely frontally. Slight tone in these drawings is used not so much for the sake of realistic light and shade as to indicate local colour. The use of tone prevents confusion in the complicated cat's-cradle of timber in Fig. 48.

However complicated scaffolding, structural wood, metal or concrete may at first appear, it *does* follow the same rules of

Fig 47

perspective as the simplest shape or body. A little analytical thought will sort it out. In Fig. 48, for instance, all horizontals – whether timbers (beams), fence or window frames – run to vanishing points on the horizon. Admittedly there are at least three vanishing points, rather than one or two as usual, but the principle is the same. Verticals of shoring (structural supports), fence, walls or windows cut across this, and serve as checks to the relative widths and proportions.

No virtue attaches to free-hand drawing as such, so there seems no reason why one should not use a ruler to aid the wobbly hand for this kind of precise drawing.

Don't let the fact that I have gone into some detail about it confirm any conviction you have that perspective is of great importance. It is not! Far happier results are possible if bogeys like vanishing points are ignored, and a free pattern is derived from the scene in front of you.

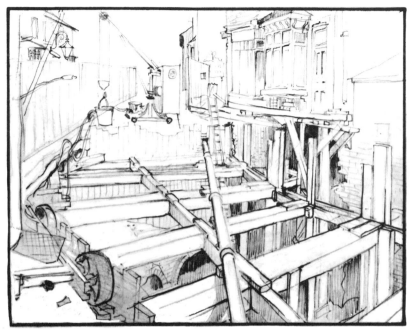

Fig 48

I have no great liking for the more ephemeral and accidental effects of atmosphere and sunlight, but occasionally cast shadows add interest and help to make a firmer and more definite pattern (Fig. 53). But the range of tone is limited in this sort of drawing, and it can only act as a diagram of light and shade. Textures of stone, wood, bricks, tiles and irregular surfaces can more success- fully be shown in pencil drawings.

If you intend using a monochrome drawing as the basis for a painting, it is advisable to include some indication of colour. A few scribbled key-words can help to recreate the scene in the studio. Reading the colour notes on the drawing, Fig. 49, brings back vividly the colours of the granite cottages of St Ives, drawn many years ago.

Colours can be indicated quite precisely. In Fig. 41, I distinguish between light grey, silver-grey, grey-green, dark grey-green and tobacco colour. Some artists carry a few coloured pencils and use these. This is nowhere near as exact; one needs to be reminded of unexpected subtleties. Red, green and blue pencils for brick, grass and sky is not enough.

The drawings discussed so far were done for study purposes, without regard for the looks or technique of the drawing. Now let

46

Fig 49 *St Ives, Cornwall*

me deal with four drawings which are more complete in themselves, and come nearer to picture-making.

Gothic churches, with their elaborate tracery and sharp angles of brackets, buttresses, arches and crockets (small ornaments), present us with complications not unlike those of scaffolding (Gothic buildings are indeed often thought of as engineering rather than as architecture). Fig. 50 is not a carefully correct drawing, but attempts to convey an impression of congested jaggedness with hardly a right-angle. Drawn with a broad-nibbed Rapidograph, there was some oil pastel added to isolate the shape of the church from the background.

In contrast Fig. 51 consists almost entirely of rectangles, even the foreground figures are nearly rectangular. Where in the last drawing most surfaces were foreshortened, here they are all square-on, parallel with the picture-plane. Drawn from an upstairs window, even the ground looks a flat, rather than a receding, surface. I used diluted black ink and my brush handle cut to a broad pen. Just as there is variation of size within the repeating rectangles of doors, windows, walls, columns and balconies, so there is changing thickness of pen line, from the spidery railings to heavy window frames. Interweaving with this linear network are

47

Fig 50 *Bridgwater, Somerset*

Fig 51   *San Vicente, Spain*

Fig 52   *Muros, Spain*

solid black rectangles, varying in size from the large doorway at the left to the patent leather hat of the policeman and the tiny window at top right.

Being drawn with a fine Rapidograph, Fig. 52 has a different feeling from the last drawing, but there are certain similarities. In spite of considerable foreshortening in the buildings, the flat pattern is stressed by means of horizontal and vertical lines and black rectangles. The figures again are rather static and are part of the formal pattern.

The roadway is the largest shape in Fig. 53, only broken by the bollards (stone posts) and the figure. The bollards do two things: first they lead the eye into the picture; second their similarity to the windows in size, shape and tone links them to the buildings and unifies the drawing. A further link is the similarity in angle between the edge of the quay and the slope of the roofs.

These abstract qualities are far more important in giving value to the drawing, than exactness of perspective or photographic naturalism.

The drawing has a more painterly approach. I used a Rapidograph, black Conté crayon and litho chalk – both are black, but

Fig 53 *Pont l'Abbé, Brittany*

Conté is soft and velvety and litho chalk is grainy, providing an interesting contrast in texture. The tone ranges from white paper in the sky to sootiest black in the windows.

But no drawing or painting can rival the range of tone seen in nature. No paper is white enough for the brilliance of the sky or a white wall in sun light, no paint dark enough to deal with a cavernous doorway. Skilful balance must determine your scale of tones. To equal the contrast in nature, the roofs ought to have been black against a white sky. But the roofs were not black. And there would have been nothing in reserve to make walls, water and, above all, the windows, darker still.

Local colour complicates the issue. The water was dark green and the sky deep blue – how can this be conveyed on a mono-chrome scale? There are no rules. Only your own judgment and sensitivity can tell you what to do.

Sometimes it simply will not work. A drawing gets darker and darker without achieving any sense of form or strength; or by overstressing a relatively unimportant part it becomes impossible to give enough emphasis to key-passages. Then is the time to scrap the drawing and to start again.

6   Wash, watercolour, gouache

The first drawing in this chapter, Fig. 54, differs from the last in the previous chapter in that a brush was used. So one could call it a painting, although no one can say exactly when a drawing turns into a painting.

It was begun with a brush-handle pen and black ink (not waterproof) and black Conté crayon. Only water was used in the brush, often while the ink was still wet, spreading it blotchily. But even dry ink will dissolve (as long as it is not waterproof) and provide some pigment; so will Conté crayon. Incidentally Conté smudges easily, but becomes smudge-proof when washed over with water.

The real subject of the drawing (or painting) is the contrast between the formal, classical bulk of the fountain and the crammed tenements behind. The windows of the houses are echoed by the stones on the edges of the fountain and the bollards (posts) along the podium and at the foot of the steps.

Fig 54   *Fountain, Rome*

Fig 55   *St Peter's, Rome*

Tone is used less to show local colour or light and shade, rather it is used to convey bulk and solidity.

The Tower of London, the sky-line of New York or St Peter's in Rome – settings like these are so hackneyed that it becomes near-impossible to see them with fresh eyes. And not only are they over-familiar. The problem is complicated by the fact that many are works of art in their own right. This further inhibits our freedom to interpret. A straight, respectful record, even a photograph, appears most appropriate.

And yet, the sense of actually being there, of recognizing what others had thought worth recording, can give one a sense of rediscovery and recognition. This is what I tried to convey in Fig. 55. There is the famed greatness of Bramante and Michelangelo, but also the bustle of tourists, the blowing spray from the fountains, the insignificant yet insistent parked cars. It is a real spot, not just a page in a book on art history – and you are actually there!

Piccadilly Circus or the Place de la Concorde would look weirdly wrong without cars, but there is always the temptation to ignore them. They get between you and the view, their shapes and colours clash with most styles of architecture – and they are not easy to draw. But they are there; probably we came in one ourselves.

One need not draw them too carefully and precisely. Like people, they move, and moreover their shapes are ephemeral and fashion-bound.

The amount of detail we can see when we concentrate on any part of a subject is greater than a drawing or painting can accommodate. For instance, the facade and dome of St Peter's is a wonderfully subtle baroque design, but if one were to try and draw all mouldings, statues and decorations, the simple and delicate shape would be drowned in a sea of detail. Time is better spent in simplifying rather than elaborating.

It is difficult to give a feeling of the size of a building if it does not have conventionally-sized details. The windows in the facade of St Peter's are at least twenty feet high, the balustrade along the top is ten feet high and the statues on it are giants of perhaps fifteen feet. Only the tiny figures in front of the church give a sense of its vastness.

The technique of the drawing is similar to that of Fig. 54; begun with a chisel-edged brush handle and black Conté, it is elaborated with blue and green washes in the foreground on the cars and barrier and some white gouache on the fountain and on the obelisk on the left.

Tourists don't flock to visit the railway footbridge in a drab South London suburb (Fig. 56), but it was as rewarding a subject as any five-starred tourist attraction. It was drawn in pen on buff Manila paper with washes in black and brown waterproof ink. The mottled sky is due to the absorbency of the paper. It serves to balance the strong vertical texture of the fence at the bottom.

The often-encountered problem of flat, featureless road surface in the foreground was solved by letting the fence take up more than half the width.

Distortions and liberties taken with the perspective help the drawing: the flattening of the background buildings, the exaggerated jaggedness of the bridge, the deviation from the vertical of lamp post and notice board. I really cannot say whether these distortions were deliberate, or whether I am being wise after the event. But as drawing and painting is always at least partly

Fig 56

instinctive and inspirational, this question is not important. What is important is that one should learn to recognize and encourage these personal and irrational impulses.

Every-day suburbia, our most familiar environment, fails to find interpreters. Only estate agents (called real estate agents in America) have their imagination stirred and find poetry in tree-lined roads of semi-detached houses. (Pop-painters do use sunburst front gates, front-door-stained-glass and plaster gnomes in their work, but this is snobbish satire.)

Fig. 58 comes as near to this subject as I have ever managed. I drew it from a parked car. What appealed to me was the elegant sweep of the descending road, echoed by the swan-like necks of the lamp posts, and the contrast of these curves with the scruffy, spiky, over-lopped trees and the related sharp gables, gates and window frames.

The drawing was started in indian ink on buff Manila paper. The first washes were near monochrome. Pink, grey and blue gouache were added and further black pen-work was put over the opaque paint.

Fig 57   *Lage, Spain*

A too-sweeping recession is arrested by the large, dark tree in the centre, and by the nearest house on the left being exactly the same tone and colour as the farthest house on the right. This provides a flat, two-dimensional tonal and colour pattern which opposes the extreme linear perspective of the converging road and lamp posts.

Figs 57 and 59 are not un-alike in subject and composition. Both are of roofs seen from above. In both, the most prominent feature is a church just off-centre, the roofs in the narrower part rising highest – in Fig. 57 on the left, in Fig. 59 on the right. I was of course not aware of repeating a previous composition so closely. I was not surprised to discover that I had done so. We all have favourite devices and preoccupations, and we revert to them time after time. But for goodness sake don't try and do it deliberately. To try and repeat previous successes is doomed to becoming an empty formula.

Fig 58 *Streatham*

Fig 59   *Rome*

However similar the compositions are, they differ in technique. Black Conté, Rapidograph and wash were used for Fig. 57. The first broad indications of the main shapes were done in Conté, then broad washes were put down to define them; the pen would then begin to clarify the smaller shapes. The three elements of the technique would come into play in turn, as first one, then the other seems indicated. It is wrong, I think, to try to complete a painting of this kind in stages, medium by medium.

Contrary to what is usually accepted, the heavier tones and stronger contrasts are at the top, the parts furthest away. This stresses the flat pattern. So do the sharp white areas with hard, black windows, spreading from the foreground to the most distant buildings.

If your work aims at illusions of atmosphere and distance, my emphasis on flat, two-dimensional pattern will serve as examples of what *not* to do.

The technique of Fig. 59 is more elaborate. Begun with a brush-handle pen and violet ink, further drawing was done in oil pastels, particularly on the roofs. Watercolour and coloured inks were added. But where I had drawn in oil pastels their greasy surface would not allow ink or watercolour to settle, so the crayon lines are unaffected. I also used gouache and further oil pastels.

Fig 60

Fig 61

Fig 62 *St Paul's, London*

Fig 63 *St Paul's, London*

The contrast between the gracious forms of St Paul's Cathedral and the meagre shapes of new office blocks and foreground are the theme of Fig. 63. My intention is clearly shown in the first stage, Fig. 60, but by the time I reached the stage shown in Fig. 61, heavy tones and textures confuse the design. In the completed painting the use of opaque paint, gouache, regains some of the initial simplicity.

I see now that I could have been bolder in the later stages and simplified further, but we are rarely as bold as we should be. The first lines on a virgin sheet of paper – or canvas – look impressively forceful. Yet when the paper is covered, these lines have shrunk into timid insignificance. One must be either careful to stop work before this early boldness is obliterated, or, and I prefer this approach, unity must be reached by simplification and overpainting.

Fig 64   *Covent Garden*

Fig 65   *Perelló, Spain*

My reason is that the artist who is intent on 'freshness' will be concerned with his deft handling of the medium rather than more important aspects – content and composition. Scared of spoiling his work, paradoxically, he will be more timid than if he accepted that he could always scratch, scrub and overpaint.

Fig. 62 was done the same morning as the previous painting, from a neighbouring roof. In the last painting grey, white, black and deep blues predominate. Here the colour is much brighter. The composition too is less stark, being based on a curve. It moves from the cross, through the dome and body of the church, left to the trees; then downwards from the trees through the blank wall, and to the right along the low triangular building, along the bus and van, and finishes bottom right.

A series of curves are the basis of Fig. 64, a pen and watercolour drawing on buff Manila paper. The theme is stated by the cupola and large semi-circular window. It is repeated in the architectural

63

detail of glazing bars (the frames which hold the panes of window glass), arched windows and arcading, the cab, headlights and wheels of the lorry (truck), the wheels and framework of the barrows, even by the curved edge of the pavement and the onion-shaped top of the lamp post. But if a drawing is too insistently composed of snaking, curving lines it becomes wearisome and self-defeating. Even a great master like Van Gogh overdid it, I think, in some of his more writhing drawings and paintings. So the vertical lines of lamp posts and flag pole, and the horizontals of the buildings, help to steady the drawing.

In contrast to the last illustration, Fig. 65 has only one curve – the path along the bottom. (Even this curve has a long straight section in the centre.) This line is the base of the upward rhythm of the painting. The higher it goes, the smaller and darker the units of the design become.

I painted this cluster of buildings from a considerable distance. They took up only a small part of my field of vision and, if you remember the discussion on page 36, you will recall my explanation of the minimal convergence to a vanishing point under these conditions. I deliberately flattened the perspective further by not letting lines converge at all.

The painting was begun with dark washes of diluted indian ink and watercolour. All light tones are subsequent layers of gouache. The gouache, which was put on fairly dry and dragged across the paper, allowed the dark background to break through in patches. Similar effects can be achieved by working in gouache (or any other opaque medium, like pastels, acrylic paint or oils) on dark, coloured paper.

7 Oils

My examples have moved from line drawings, through more tonal drawings to wash, and finally to paintings done with opaque pigments.

It is a short step from there to oils. It is appropriate then to start with an oil painting here, Fig. 66, of the same Spanish village as the final gouache in the last chapter (Fig. 65). Individual buildings have little interest or distinction. It is this box-like simplicity that makes a good pattern from clusters of them. So it may be no coincidence that Picasso painted his first Cubist

Fig 66 *Perelló, Spain*

pictures of farms and factories in this part of Spain.

Contrasting tones and shapes echo each other in my painting. The dark, round arch under the road is balanced by the light, angular gable-end above it. The light rectangles of the concrete blocks edging the road are related to the dark windows and chimneys. The light slopes of road embankment and buttresses in the foreground run counter to the predominant slope of the dark roofs in the right half of the painting.

If you turn the book upside down, this abstract aspect of the composition becomes even clearer. This is a useful device. If any part of your painting seems wrong, turning it upside down may well show you where the fault lies. Not only does doing so show abstract qualities. Oddly enough, it also reveals weaknesses in perspective or a lack of solidity. Looking at your painting in a mirror will similarly expose faulty drawing and unintentional distortions. But this will only work the first time. As you become familiar with the mirror-image of the painting, it loses its value as a detector. And here I will mention a third self-critical device: half-close your eyes to analyse tonal relationships and to eliminate distracting detail in nature or in your painting. The more narrowly you blink between closing lids, the more will detail and colour disappear.

To be more than an impersonal record, a painting must have some additional quality. This can be a matter of composition, as here. Or the colour can be heightened. The brushwork can express emotional turmoil – think of paintings of street scenes and churches by Van Gogh and Soutine.

These personal, subjective interpretations, additions, distortions, simplifications, will be different for every artist. If a dozen painters paint the same scene, there will be twelve different scenes. And even if the same artist paints the same subject over and over, each time he will discover new aspects.

But the artist's individual choice begins earlier; with his decision of *what* to paint, from what angle, how big, and how much of it to include in his painting. The last point will partly be decided by your field of vision. Do not include more in the painting than you can comfortably see without moving head or eyes – roughly a fifteen-inch diameter at arms length.

Two considerations should help further. First, you should recognize what it is essential to include, the parts that made you think the subject worth painting. Secondly, and most importantly, what will make a satisfactory composition. Related to this is your choice of format – upright, oblong, square or narrow.

Fig 67

Fig 68

Fig 69

Fig 70

Making a few compositional diagrams (Figs 67, 68, 69, 70), before embarking on the painting can save regrets and hours of work. If you are pleased with one of these preliminary scribbles and decide to base your painting on it, it is important to adhere very closely to its proportions in the painting. For instance, the deep band of the foreground is very much part of the composition in Fig. 70.

The coarse brushwork, inconsistent perspective and clumsy detail of Fig. 71 is deliberate. It is used to convey the air of neglect and the heavy, rather congested feeling that the church gave with its squat tower and steeple.

Cold and harsh colours are used: dark greys, greenish grey, black, prussian blue in the church, a near-white, colourless sky and a blue-grey foreground.

Fig. 72 is a painting of the same church, now seen from beyond the edge of the town. Crowding all detail into the upper half and leaving more than half the picture space empty, gives a feeling of the contrast between the enclosed town and the open country beyond. The painting avoids falling into two halves by the use of the jagged texture of the grass in the foreground, which repeats the pointed rhythm of the roofs, tower, belfry and pinnacles.

You will have noticed that in some of my paintings I use heavy outlines. Clearly, there are no outlines in nature. So, if you are intent on photographic illusionism, you will avoid them. But I do hope that you do not think the aim of art is the copying of optical sensations. My use of line can be explained by the fact that at the time when I did these paintings, several years ago, I also did a lot of bold line drawings. These influenced my paintings. Only as I became aware of these lines becoming a mannerism, did I gradually wean myself of the device.

Fig 71   *Penmarc, Brittany*

Fig 72   *Penmarc, Brittany*

Never fear that by discarding a mannerism you will lose your style and personality. By the time you are aware of it, it has ceased to be a style and has become an empty formula.

If you do use lines, try to let them grow with the painting. Do not begin with a line drawing done with a brush and then fill in the blank areas with paint, carefully leaving the lines showing. And don't put heavy lines around the shapes as the last stage of your picture.

Fig 73 *Newport, Monmouthshire*

Fig 74

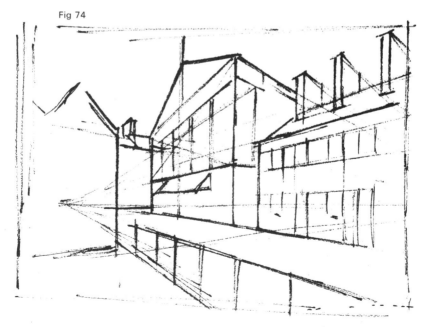

Fig. 73 was painted as a record of a building doomed to demolition, in suitably sombre colours – black, grey, yellow ochre and brown. Being a record, the composition is simple and sober.

As I was a good distance from the buildings, the foreshortening is not insistent, perspective only slightly raising its ugly head. If I had been closer it would have looked more like Fig. 74, distorting the pleasant proportions of the building and putting undue emphasis on the foreground.

Scale is provided by the small houses, which make the Victorian theatre loom large. The big, blunt shapes against the sky-line become thinner and scratchier as they get nearer ground-level, ending with the spidery grid of the barrier. I deliberately excluded people or traffic, to give a forlorn look to the scene.

I began the painting perched on the roof of my car in the empty car park (parking lot) one week-end. It was completed in the studio, taking many hours of work. Time spent is not necessarily apparent in the amount of detail. The painting is in fact now much freer and simpler than in some of the earlier stages. This gradual process encourages a more considered balance of tones and shapes than a quick impression is likely to have. Also, the layers of paint impart a richness and denseness of surface which cannot be achieved in any other way.

It had been my view from the studio window for several years when I did the painting in Fig. 75. The old men were propped against the ledge for hours every day; I knew every brick. Something of one's affection and understanding creeps into the painting of a familiar scene. But that aspect is so personal that it cannot usefully be analysed. So if I write mainly about the more impersonal aspects of composition, colour and technique, it does not mean that there is nothing else to be expressed in a painting.

The painting divides vertically into two near-equal parts: the front of the house on the left and the view along the road on the right. Showing part of the building only on the left, gives greater importance to the details of shop front, window and figures and a sense of intimacy which, for instance, the previous painting does not have.

Painted quite thinly, only the light patches are in heavy impasto. Grey and terracotta predominate; grey on the left, terracotta on the right. Making the background at top right the warmest colour brings it optically forward. In order to unify the composition I have gone contrary to the accepted realistic rule (distance=cool colour).

Fig 75 *Halesowen, Worcestershire*

Apart from artistic considerations, painting on your home ground has advantages. There is no need to spend time travelling, no problem of carrying canvases and materials or of possible wet weather, no curious bystanders to ignore.

But you may feel that the views from your house were especially created to be unpaintable. Nothing could, I think, look less rewarding than our London backyard. Yet it made at least one painting, Fig. 79. Its interest lies in the contrast between the receding and bending screen of buildings and the rigid slabs of fence and wall parallel with the picture plane.

In Fig. 76, an early stage of the painting, there is confusion about the various planes. The edge of the roofs against the sky is also blunt and clumsy. Ultimately the light grass in the fore-

Fig. 76

ground and the white wall and washing clarified the composition. Although all buildings are more or less the same colour, the more distant ones recede, because their windows are painted in less contrasting tones. The figures and swing not only add incident, but prevent the lower half consisting entirely of horizontals.

Fig. 77 is a street in North London – slum dwellings, a tin-roofed garage and, in the foreground, a gas-repair gang's handcart. It rained so hard whilst I painted it, from the car, that I had to keep the windscreen (windshield) wipers going. Fig. 78 was painted in the court of Trinity College on a fine May morning.

Fig 77 (opposite)   *Finsbury*

Fig 78   *Trinity College, Cambridge*

Yet the two paintings are similar in many essentials: the rhythm of chimneys and turrets; the rows of windows; the horizontal lines at ground and roof levels; the gateway in Cambridge one third from the left, as is the light front of the work-shop in Fig. 77. There is similarity too in the foreground shapes on the left: a Tudor fountain in one, a handcart in the other.

Exaggeratedly wide (or tall) paintings, like Fig. 78, are regarded with suspicion. A proportion of 3:4, or at most 2:3, is usually thought proper. There have of course been exceptions to this, from Egyptian friezes and oriental scroll paintings to Picasso's *Guernica*, and Cinerama. But on the whole I think it a sensible rule. Firstly because our field of vision is more or less as high as it is wide, and therefore a near-square painting can be seen more easily as a unit; and secondly because there are more subtle compositions possible within these conventional proportions.

Fig. 78 was in fact begun in a more usual format, but after a great deal of repainting and unsuccessful changes I chopped off a lot of foreground, a drastic, but sometimes necessary, operation.

Fig 79

8   Painting from drawings

The Impressionists a hundred years ago were the first to take oil paint and canvas out-of-doors. Their concern was with light and colour, in a scientific spirit.

Before 1860 nearly all painting had been done from preparatory sketches. For one thing, painting techniques as practised then (tempera and oil), were so elaborate and time-consuming that it would have been impossible to practise them out-of-doors. For another, painters then thought that only deliberately worked out compositions had real value. (Even Constable only exhibited work which he had done in the studio from preliminary studies.)

Although few artists today use painstaking and elaborate techniques, the point about the importance of composition is still true.

When nature confronts me I find myself overwhelmed by colour, movement, detail, changing light and sensations of depth and distance. Paradoxically perhaps, it is easier to cope with all this in a drawing, where your means – line and monochrome – are limited and clearly cannot interpret all you see, than in a painting, where more elaborate means and colour are available.

In a drawing, one can resolve the complications of three-dimensional reality into a linear, flat pattern. If one is too preoccupied with perspective in a painting, it can be distracting.

Shadows and cast shadows are constantly moving and, at least in England, are likely to be wiped out at a moment's notice by clouds. In a swift drawing one can cope with them, when a painting, being so much slower, will fail.

The following examples illustrate most of these points.

Fig. 80 was begun on a left-hand page and gradually sprawled across both sketch-book pages. Standing on a traffic island with traffic passing on either side, I was literally in no position for lengthy contemplation. It was days later that I decided to use only the right half of the drawing for an upright painting (Fig. 82). The device of letting the buildings take up only a third, with empty space above and below, was hinted at by the accidental placing on the sketch-book page. The thing which may have decided my choice of which part to use may have been the indication of the most dominant patch of colour – yellow ochre.

As the painting progressed, tones and colours gradually became paler, and finally this yellow ochre patch was lost, as I felt that the dark to the left of it gave enough emphasis to the centre of the composition.

The beer poster became a blank wall. I simplified buttresses, out-buildings and roof levels in the centre. On the other hand I

Fig 80 *Kings Cross Road, London*

brought the lamp post from the left half of the drawing and put it across the blank wall. This was done to balance the shoring timbers (structural beams) and high wall on the right.

Two kinds of textures are used: linear – directly influenced by the drawing – put on with a sable brush; across the low wall in front, on chimneys and dark outbuildings in the centre. And secondly, glazes and scumbles. (Glazes are transparent washes, darker than the background, scumbles are washes of colour lighter than the background. For glazes transparent colours are used, such as burnt umber, raw and burnt sienna, the madders, alizarin crimson, viridian and prussian blue. For scumbles opaque colours, often containing white, are usual. Generally speaking, glazes add warmth to a picture, scumbles turn it cool.)

Splashy brown glazes – burnt umber – are on the foreground, and there are white scumbles, heavy on the blank wall on the left and thin on sky and buildings on the right. These thin layers of paint add to the misty delicacy of tone and colour.

There were dogs around my feet, children playing, people coming and going on the benches, and boats moving on the river when I drew Fig. 40 (page 39). I could have ignored all this, as I ignored the traffic in Figs 73 and 82, but it seemed such an essential part of the edge-of-river scene.

Not only are the figures and dog repositioned in the painting (Fig. 81), the setting itself is changed. The light building on the right is nearer to the dark house, the railings at the river's edge and behind the bench are changed; so is the position of the bench.

Fig 81

Fig 82

Colour is used unrealistically. Whatever colour the river Thames is, it is not white, nor is the river-side path. These light tones and the ones of the building at top right set off the darks which move across the painting – from the railings behind the bench, through the dark building, the two trees and the horizontal girders of the railway bridge. The dark and light coats of the two women echo the dark and light buildings behind them.

The tonal scheme of the painting was suggested by the slight indications on the drawing, where the trees and the building are lightly shaded and one of the figures on the far right has tone on her coat.

The cloistered atmosphere of the Breton church square made me want to draw it (Fig. 83). A near-symmetrical view – church on left, priest's house on right – seemed to suit the subject. There is no good reason why a painting should not be symmetrical. Some of the most beautiful things in nature and art are symmetrical, from the human body to a Gothic cathedral.

I did the drawing with a Rapidograph in late afternoon on a hot day, as the shadows were rapidly lengthening across the dusty ground. What had looked in nature a compact, enclosed area, in the drawing began to look a long and narrow space, high buildings on either side, tiny ones ahead. This is an example of the fact that what to our sense of space is an exciting setting, so often translates on paper into the disappointingly commonplace. It is stereoscopic vision which fools us. But by closing one eye it is possible to have a better appreciation of what a scene will look like when translated into a drawing or painting. And look-ing at a scene with one eye through a view-finder (either your thumb and forefinger making a frame, or through a rectangle cut out of a piece of paper), will also help you to plan the composition of your picture.

When I came across the sketch months later I felt that, in spite of its shortcomings, it had possibilities. This is a further advantage of working from drawings. Sketches done on a few weeks' holiday can be raw material for months – even years – of painting.

In the painting (Fig. 84) I did several things to give the sense of enclosure which the drawing could not convey. I enlarged and raised the buildings in the middle, bringing the strongest tonal contrast – the triangular roof against the light wall – into the exact centre of the painting. Broken and neutral tones reduce the importance of the high buildings at left and right. I kept the sense of strong light falling from the right, but eliminated the confusing edge of the cast shadow on the ground. I simplified the tones.

Fig 83   *Guilvinec, Brittany*

Fig 84

Basically there are now only three: 1, the light parts of the buildings; 2, the darker parts of buildings, sky and ground; 3, near-black roofs, windows and figures. Compare this with the confusion of tones in the drawing.

I simplified the church on the left, feeling that there should not be too much fussy detail in any one part. But the figures of the two priests are in the same position, and some inconsistencies in perspective are carried into the painting.

All parallel converging lines – along the church roof, at the foot and top of the wall etc. – should, but do not, meet in one vanishing point somewhere on the far wall. I was not deliberately inconsistent when I did the drawing. Whatever the initial cause – carelessness, accident or artistic instinct – it was consciously used in the painting. There can be a dullness, a smoothly-theoretical look, about constructed perspective.

Artists take liberties with many aspects of the seen world: colour, treatment (such as putting lines around objects), simplification. There is no reason why they should abide by the rules of perspective. If art were an objective science, there could be universally-accepted laws. But since art is so essentially personal, since no two artists can ever agree what makes a good drawing, for instance, there are no rules to be broken.

Having been commissioned to paint a panoramic view of Cambridge, I obtained permission to do some drawings (title page) from the University Press tower. Apart from the impossibility of dragging a large board up there; the painting is five feet wide; I should not have liked to tackle this subject on the spot. There was the problem of turning a complicated three-dimensional patchwork like a town in bird's-eye-view into a solid and balanced composition. This is further complicated by the distracting changes in light which are bound to occur in the long time an elaborate and large painting takes.

After spending a solid day drawing on the roof, my impressions were still fresh when I began the painting (Fig. 85), on the following day. Drawing anything is a tremendous help in recalling its details and colours later on. Even without reference to the drawing, it is possible to do a painting of it days later, an otherwise quite impossible undertaking.

Some sparkle and spontaneous vividness which drawings and direct paintings can have is often lost in the ultimate painting, but it can have qualities of greater value. In this case, for instance, the unconvincing perspective of the road on the right has been steadied and turned into a more interesting shape; the foreground

Fig 85 *Cambridge*

roofs to the right of centre have been changed into a more inventive series of shapes, and so have the roofs to the right of the road. There is now strength in the pattern of windows and chimneys in the centre of the painting, which is lacking in the drawing.

In architectural subjects there are sequences of repeating units. They can be small – bricks, tiles or stones; they can be larger – windows, chimneys, crenellations; they can even be rows of identical houses. You may feel that unless you vary these repeating shapes you will produce a dull painting. (I confess that I frequently suffer from that feeling.) You can see in several of my paintings here, and particularly in the present one, how I tried to overcome this, by varying tone, colour, thickness of line and amount of detail. Do not take too much note of this. I could cite many instances of artists, from Canaletto to Lowry, who were content to paint monotonously-regular rows of chimneys, windows or bricks and yet produced exciting paintings.

One part I found particularly difficult; the transition from foreground to middle distance and then from middle distance to background. The reason is that we see these three elements in three different ways. In the foreground we see shapes as bulky three-dimensional solids. In the middle distance they become flat, but well-defined areas. In the background, even on a clear day, shapes are vague and become an indefinite horizontal texture.

Aerial perspective will affect tones and colours. The nearer the object, the truer will its colour appear and the stronger will be tonal contrasts; the further away, the less contrast will there be in tone and colour. The pervading colour will depend on the weather and time of day. The distant colours can be blue-tinged, purple, grey or, towards sunset, even gold or pink.

9 Interiors

The problems of interiors are no different from those of exterior views. Composition is as important, light falls in the same way, perspective does the same to the inside of a box as to its outside.

A vast view of the nave of a cathedral, with pillars, vaulting and tracery, is an interior. So is the bit of wall behind a still life or a portrait.

More than with other subjects there is the temptation to take too wide an angle of vision, to include too much of what is above (the ceiling or roof), to show too much of what is below (the floor) and to go too far on left and right. Not only does one tend to do so wanting to convey a sense of enclosure, but the distortion is much more easily recognized. In a landscape or a street scene the top of the painting will usually be sky, and even if a high and wide expanse of sky is included, there is no sense of distortion. Nor is grass or earth underfoot a give-away, as are tiles or floor-boards.

Artists have often tried to include more in their paintings than one can see without moving head or eye. In the centre of Van Eyck's Arnolfini portrait, painted in about 1430, there is a tiny convex mirror reflecting the whole of the room. Kokoschka's townscapes take in a vast sweep, far beyond what one can see in one glance. Science imitates art in the photographs taken with wide-angle and fish-eye lenses, which bend perspective and show more than the human eye can take in.

The Spanish beach café (Fig. 86), deserted at Easter, was as simple as a child's drawing of a house. The hut at the right echoes the skeletal structure which shelters tables and benches. It is exterior and interior at the same time. Like a greenhouse with glass walls, you see inside and outside simultaneously.

We may be annoyed at the spoiling of a bit of beach, or pleased to get a drink or a cup of tea. It needs a second look to realize that a flimsy shack can be the source of a painting. Look at the pattern made by the lattice of tables, benches and poles cutting across each other. The proportions and angles of these segments are as subtle and refined as those of an abstract painting by Mondrian or Ben Nicholson.

And again the oil painting, Fig. 87, is not an interior in the usual sense, but the cross roads under the railway bridge have all the essential characteristics: roof, confining walls and light breaking into dark space.

Although I am not displeased with my painting (I even managed to sell it!), it will serve to point out two easily-committed

Fig 86

mistakes. Trying to show as much as possible of the scene, I took in a wide, possibly too wide, angle. The fiercely spreading perspective in the overhead structure is due to this. As a side effect it makes the space look deeper and loftier than it really is.

Secondly, if one attempts to give a feeling of light against a dark inside space, detail, contrast and definition within both dark and light areas must be sacrificed. I was too interested in the structure and texture of my subject to heed this.

Half-close your eyes and look at a window and wall around it. All detail disappears, and only the light shape of the window against a flat, dark background remains. This will demonstrate that the darkest in the light is far lighter than the lightest in the dark.

I do not advocate that you follow this in your painting, but you cannot expect to have both – a realistic effect of light and shade, and equal emphasis on detail throughout.

Fig 87 *Kings Cross*

My pen, wash and chalk drawing of an Irish bar (Fig. 88), however different the subject, illustrates similar points. Again my interest in detail and texture has led me to stress this at the expense of tonal unity. And again there is a wide visual angle. Here it is vertical, from the ceiling to the barrel at my feet.

On the other hand, in the watercolour, Fig. 89, I was concerned with the effects of light and shade. Therefore detail was kept to a minimum. Tone, too, had to be simplified for convincing effect. The difference between the lightest tone, the sky, and the tracery of branches is greater in nature than the contrast between white paper and black paint. But the contrast between these branches and the darkest tone indoors is nearly as great again. So the scale of tone available to you on your sheet of paper is perhaps only a quarter of the range in the scene. It is up to your judgment how you use the means at your disposal. You can, as I do here, use tone to stress the outside light – inside dark effect. Or, as in other examples, you can concentrate on colour, solidity, line or detail.

Fig 88   *Irish bar*

Fig 89

Fig 90   *Spanish kitchen*

The less of a room one paints, the more successful is the feeling of enclosed space and intimacy. Think of the interiors by seventeenth-century painters, such as Vermeer and De Hooch. They hardly ever show more than a bit of one wall and a little of the floor, occasionally part of a window on one side or a door opening into a passage.

I had the source of light behind me when I drew Fig. 90, so there were no dramatic shadows. And as I only drew a narrow section of what I saw, the 'wide-angle' problem of previous examples was also avoided. It was a simple subject. Wall and stove are parallel with the picture plane. The horizontal and vertical lines of the stylized, exaggeratedly-tilted floor continue the grid of wall-tiles and stove. I am in trouble though at the left, where the recession of sink and wall has to be treated more realistically. Fortunately the curtain and chair disguise this inconsistency in perspective.

The drawing is on deep yellow paper with pen, wash and white gouache on the tiles. Thinking that the tiles on wall, stove and floor were dull and repetitive, I tried to vary their tone and texture, unnecessarily perhaps. Chair, curtain, still-life objects and the iron stove would have been enough to give interest.

Fig 91   *Dr Cartwright, Mistress of Girton College, Cambridge*

In street scenes and most interiors, figures play a subordinate part. In a portrait the individual is the most important part, but he need not fill the picture. Just as an individual's clothes are an expression of his personality, so is his setting. Contrived or invented curtains, book shelves and views through windows are no better than the Victorian photographer's plaster pillars, canvas rocks and aspidistra. But as often as not portraits are painted in one's studio, rather than in the sitter's home. It can then be painted frankly against your background, rather than the sitter's. Or it may be possible for you to do some preliminary studies in the sitter's home and to incorporate the background when you paint the figure in the studio. This may be cumbersome and tricky, but it is quite possible, as the following example (Fig. 91), shows.

The drawing was casual, but in the painting I stress the architectural, structural character of the composition. The settee is squarer, detail on the table and on the right is simplified, heavy outlines, the dark curtain and window frame emphasize the structure. The composition progresses from the *single* most important unit, the figure, to the settee, which is divided vertically into *two*,

Fig 92

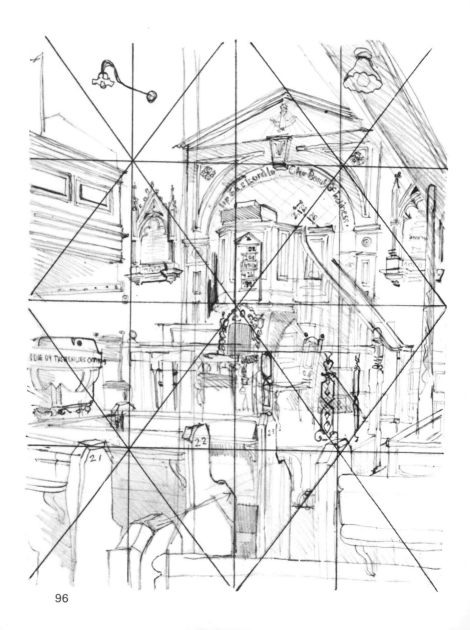

then to the *four* units of window and curtain, finally to the many small units of dormers, windows and chimneys seen through the window.

Although the figure does not take up a large area, and in spite of its not being in the centre, it is the focus.

Not only the setting, but the placing of the model can be an expression of character. The position of the figure and the subdued colours – greys, browns, dusty pink – are in keeping with the sitter's restrained personality.

The interiors of a church and of a non-conformist chapel, Figs 92 and 93, drawn in pencil, are preliminary sketches for black and white illustrations. The book was on architecture, therefore although I was not obliged to show everything in great detail, the drawings had to convey objective information.

These preliminary drawings were for my own information. Like shorthand notes, only the artist himself has to be able to read them. Where units repeat themselves I only indicated one of them in the sketches, such as the tiles and the tracery on the rood screen in Fig. 92, and the iron castings of the communion rail and the pattern on the arch behind the pulpit in Fig. 93. Indications of tone are similarly diagrammatic. In the church, tone was important in the dark roof-spaces and in the silhouetted tracery of the windows. The chapel was lighted more evenly, and shadows play a smaller part. Pattern, texture and local colour – the actual colours of paintwork, upholstery and timber – are therefore stressed.

The network of diagonal, horizontal and vertical lines was used to transfer the drawing on to a sheet of board for the finished illustration. So as not to confuse the already complicated drawing further, these lines were here drawn in coloured pencil.

Fig 93

10 Painting from photographs

There is essentially little difference whether you paint directly from the subject, from a drawing or from a photograph. The fact that a photograph is a ready-made, two-dimensional record of a scene in the round does not make your task much easier – you must interpret, not copy. Before you can use the photograph you have to reconstitute in your mind the flat print into three-dimensional reality. The fact that the camera solves problems of perspective and foreshortening does not automatically help to paint better pictures. On the contrary, it is the very struggle with these problems that adds conviction and reveals personality in a painting.

All the same, photographs can be of use. They will record a fleeting effect of light or movement which is beyond the quickest drawer.

If you only have time or patience to do a very rough sketch of an ornate and complicated subject, a photograph you take of it (or even a postcard) can help with a subsequent more elaborate painting. But I have found, whenever I have done this, that the drawing, however summary, was of far more use than the sharpest photograph.

The camera can record effects of light and shade. I have, for instance, used photographs of streets at night as references for paintings.

A photograph will record a fleeting effect of light or movement.

Many splendid photographs are reproduced in the press. Often they are considerable works of art in their own right and so good that they leave no scope for further interpretation. Others may be of scenes or places which appeal to you and which you are unlikely to see in reality. I have, for instance, seen photographs of Mexican churches which I felt would make good paintings.

The most ordinary photographs are the most fruitful. A casual snapshot may suddenly reveal itself to you as containing elements of composition, or evoke an atmosphere which demands translation into paint. My example does not quite fall into this category. When I took the photograph in Fig. 94, I did suspect that it might serve for a painting.

By eliminating the foreground tree, it became apparent that the blunt vertical column on the left and the horizontal bulk of the trees on the other side of the Tiber would dominate the composition. I had intended to paint the buildings very simply and block-like (Fig. 95), but they loomed too importantly. So, following the photograph more closely than I had intended, I broke the buildings up with textures and details of windows and

Fig 94 *Lungotevere Sanzio, Rome*

mouldings. The figures were also too insistent and competed with the column. Departing from the tonal scheme of the photograph and darkening the road, I unified road and men into one shape. Stippling the trees not only gave them leaves; more important, it brought them forward into the picture plane.

Although I did paint a square picture from a square photograph, there is clearly no need to use the whole of a photoprint, or

Fig 95

to keep to its proportions.

As a matter of personal taste I like high horizons. So not only did I pick a photograph with a lot of foreground, but I further reduced the depth of the sky. Buildings only take up a small part of the painting, but people, roads, railings, and traffic signs are as much a part of town.

Fig 96

To *copy* a photograph is pointless, but there is nothing to feel guilty about if you use the photograph – or anything else - as a starting-off point. Utrillo painted from picture-postcards, but look what he made of them! Van Gogh used Japanese woodcuts, Victorian book illustrations, photographs, Rembrandt paintings and an old pair of boots, and turned them all into Van Gogh's.

101

Further study

Few books are specifically concerned with the artist in the town. Books for architects on drawing perspective-views of planned buildings may be of some use to you. The most lively and far-ranging book of this kind is *The Perspectivist* by R. Myerscough-Walker, published by Pitman in 1958.

There are of course many excellent books on the history of architecture. Banister Fletcher's *Comparative Architecture*, although first published in 1896, is still useful, gathering a vast amount of information in one volume.

In England we are fortunate to have Nikolaus Pevsner's *The Buildings of England*, published by Penguin, a series which surveys the whole country. But these books are for the person interested in architecture, rather than for the painter.

Of most interest and profit may be the study of painters who have dealt with the subject. Excellent volumes are available on the following:

Piero della Francesca
Vermeer
Dürer
Canaletto
Van Gogh
Cézanne
Derain
Kokoschka

There are many books on these modern artists:

Utrillo
Sickert
Feininger
Soutine
Edward Hopper
Lowry

The Fauves, published by Thames & Hudson, contains many examples of townscapes by Matisse, Dufy, Braque and Vlaminck.

Many volumes are published on the English watercolour-painters of the late eighteenth and early nineteenth century, such as Bonnington, Boys and Cox.

Index